THE BIG BOOK OF READING COMPREHENSION ACTIVITIES, GRADE 1

The Big Book of
Reading Comprehension Activities

GRADE 1

120 Activities for After-School and Summer Reading Fun

Hannah Braun, MEd

Illustrations by Joel and Ashley Selby

ZEPHYROS
PRESS

Cover and Interior Designer: William Mack
Art Manager: Sue "Bees" Bischofberger
Editor: Katharine Moore
Production Editor: Erum Khan
Illustrations © 2019 Joel and Ashley Selby

ISBN: Print 978-1-64152-294-6

Contents

Letter to Parents and Teachers

I'm Hannah, a former teacher and mom of two. If you picked up this book, I bet you love it when a child lights up because they made a connection, answered their own question, or got the joke in something they read. That sense of accomplishment is thrilling for both the child and the adult!

Reading comprehension standards can feel like a long list of disjointed skills. The truth is, comprehension boils down to something very simple: Authors write so that readers will take something away from their text. All reading comprehension practice should be aimed at uncovering the author's message.

You're in a position to help kids go from "word calling" to pulling meaning out of a text. It might be a life lesson, a new opinion to consider, a better understanding of something, or a good laugh. This juncture in the learning process is a powerful place to be! I'm excited to walk with you on a path to better reading comprehension for your child or students.

I based the readings and activities in this book on the following research-based principles:

- Children construct meaning as they read by connecting new ideas with their prior knowledge.
- Children benefit from exposure to a wide variety of text, including narratives, nonfiction, poetry, and opinion pieces.
- Awareness of common text structures helps children know what to expect as they read.
- Children can be taught how to read strategically.
- Mastery of a skill happens after multiple opportunities to practice it.

The activities in this book are designed to be completed with adult help. To get the most out of the activities, try the following:

- Provide more assistance with decoding words than you might normally. This allows the child to really focus on the targeted comprehension skill.

- If the child needs more support, read the passages aloud to them or read chorally (your voice and the child's voice together).
- Have the child reread parts of passages as needed to help them complete an activity.
- Demonstrate your thinking. If a child is stuck on an activity, show how you, as a proficient reader, would approach it. Use phrases like, "I noticed...", "I wonder...", or "This makes me think..."

For an additional challenge, extend the passages by asking questions like these:

- What is another way the story could have ended?
- What does that remind you of?
- How does that make you feel?
- Does this change your thinking?
- What would you do if you were in this story?
- What surprised you?

The readings and activities in this book start out easy and get more challenging as the book goes on. You can begin at the front and advance through the activities in order to help your child or students build up their skills. Alternatively, if you want to focus on a specific comprehension skill, use the skills index in the back of the book (see page 128) to jump to an appropriate activity—this index also includes correlations to Common Core standards.

Best of luck to you as you guide your child or students toward reading comprehension success!

120 Reading Comprehension Activities

LIFE WITH CECE

Tim was mad at Cece. When Tim played, Cece played, too.

When Tim ate, Cece ate, too. It was hard to live with Cece.

But when Cece felt sad, Tim felt sad, too.

Mark each sentence below by coloring in the check if it's true, or the X if it's false. Hint: Use information from both the words and the pictures to help you.

1. Cece is an adult.   ✓ ✗

2. Cece gets in Tim's way.   ✓ ✗

3. Tim has building blocks.   ✓ ✗

4. Cece leaves Tim alone.   ✓ ✗

SKILL Use illustrations to describe characters, settings, and events

THE LITTLE HEN

"Will you help me pick the apples?"

"No, I will not."

"Will you help me cut the apples?"

"No, I will not."

"Will you help me bake the pie?"

"No, I will not."

"We will help you eat the pie!"

"No, you will not!"

1. Draw an arrow to the animal who would not cut the apples.
2. Draw an X near the animal who would not pick the apples.
3. Draw a circle around each animal who wanted to eat the pie.
4. Draw a square around the animal who did all the work.

SKILL Use illustrations to describe characters, settings, and events

SAM'S HIDEOUT

This is my castle. I made it myself. I can see a dragon outside of my castle. I can see a bridge outside of my castle. I can see a tree outside of my castle. I can see a river outside of my castle.

"Sam, where are you?"

"I'm by my castle, Mom!"

Circle the word that completes each sentence. Use the picture to help you.

1. The story is really happening outside a _____.   [castle / blanket fort]

2. The dragon is really _____.   [dangerous / a toy]

3. Sam is really _____.   [a boy / a king]

4. Sam is _____.   [imagining / a real prince]

SKILL Use illustrations to describe characters, settings, and events

WHERE IS MISSY?

I find my cat, Missy, in many places. Once she was hiding up high. She was sleeping.

Once she was hiding down low. She was sleeping.

Once she was hiding in between. She was sleeping. Missy can sleep anywhere!

Write where the story is happening on the blank line. Then write or draw three things you could see if you went to the place. Use details in the pictures above.

The story is happening at a _____.

SKILL Use illustrations to describe characters, settings, and events

A NEW FRIEND FOR LEX

Lex saw something new. He stopped to look. It was a dog! Lex sat down. The other dog sat down, too.

Lex waved his paw. The other dog waved his paw, too.

Lex walked away. The other dog walked away, too. "What a nice dog he was," Lex said to himself.

Use the clues to complete the crossword puzzle.

1. Lex is really looking into a _____.

2. Lex thinks he sees a different _____.

3. How many dogs are really in the story?

4. Lex says the other dog is _____.

LUNCH BUNCH

It was lunchtime for Cam's class. He sat with his friends.

Jun had a sandwich . Nan had a hot dog. They told jokes.

Soon, it was time to go play outside.

Characters are the people, animals, or other beings that the story is about. Complete the gallery below by drawing a picture of each character in the story and writing their name.

SKILL Answer questions about key details

CREATURE CHARACTERS

"Help me!" said the crab. "I want to make a sandcastle."

"I can dig up sand," said the turtle.

"I can slap at the sand," said the seal.

"I can put a twig on top," said the snail. Each animal helped build the castle.

Sometimes characters are animals or other creatures. Circle the pictures that show characters from this story.

SKILL Answer questions about key details

THE BEST SPOT

From the car I saw lots of tall trees. We were driving up

a mountain  . We stopped in a dirt lot. I helped my

dad get the fishing poles   out. We walked to a lake

and sat on big rocks.

My dad said, "Lazy Lake is the best spot to catch fish!"

The setting is where the story is happening. Using details from the story, design a postcard to match the setting. Write the name of the place and draw what it looks like.

GREETINGS *from*

BAD NEWS BIRTHDAY

It was Fin's birthday . She was having a party in the park later. There would be games and food. Fin heard a boom! She went outside. The sky was cloudy . She felt a drop of rain. "Oh no," thought Fin. "How will we have a party now? It will be too wet at the park."

In most stories, the character faces a problem or something that goes wrong. Fill in the blanks below to help Fin describe her problem in this story.

I wanted to have

a _____.

It might get ruined because of

the _____.

I wish the weather

was _____.

A TREAT IN THE TREE

Vic was making something for the birds. First, he got a pine cone .

Next, he spread peanut butter all over the pine cone. Then, he

put birdseed on the sticky pine cone. He put some string on it.

Last, he hung the pine cone treat in a tree so the birds could eat it.

Start at the star. Draw lines to connect the pictures in the order that story events happened. Some pictures will not be used.

START

SKILL Answer questions about key details

EYES UP HIGH

Adam Ant lost his hat. He looked under a leaf. Not there. He looked by a rock. Not there. He looked in the grass. Not there. Adam sat in the dirt, feeling sad.

"Look up!" said Sal Spider. Adam looked up. His hat was stuck in Sal's web! Sal climbed down and put the hat back on Adam's head.

Stories have a beginning, a middle, and an end. Use the lines beneath the pictures to label them with a B for beginning, an M for middle, and an E for end to match the story events. Can you use the pictures to tell someone else the story events in order?

_____   _____   _____

SKILL Retell stories and demonstrate an understanding of their lesson

BIKE RIDE SIGHTS

"Let's go!" said Sho. She and her mom were going on a bike ride.

They went by the park. Kids were playing. Then they went over

a bridge  . Last, they went by a pond.

"I feel tired now," said Mom. "Let's go home." It was a great ride!

Complete the picture below by drawing in the things Sho and her mom saw on their ride in the correct order. Look back at the text for help if you need it. Can you use the picture to tell someone else the story events in order?

SKILL Retell stories and demonstrate an understanding of their lesson

BOX PILOT

A big box came to my house. When the box was empty, Mom let me

have it. I cut paper to give the box wings. I used crayons

to give the box windows. I put in a pillow to give the box a seat.

I got inside my box plane and played!

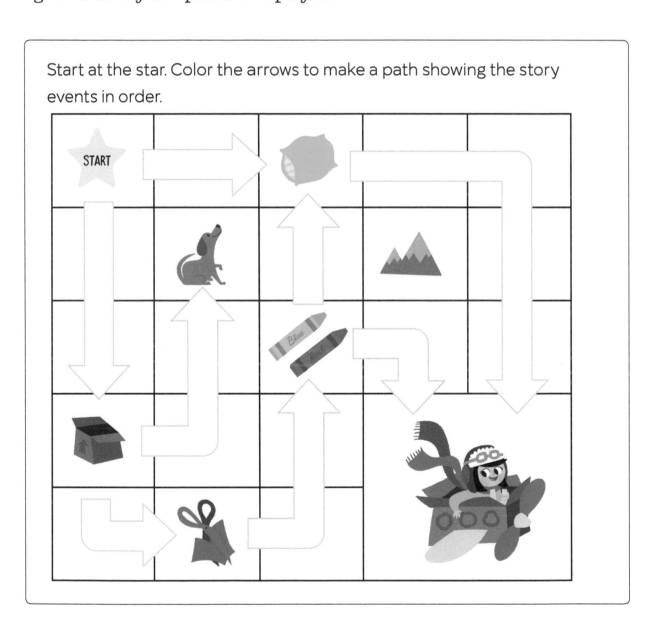

Start at the star. Color the arrows to make a path showing the story events in order.

SKILL Retell stories and demonstrate an understanding of their lesson

THE NEW FROG

Ben saw a new frog in the pond.

"Look at his hat," said Ben. "Look at his glasses ⊙⊙ . He does not look like the other frogs. I will stay away from him." Then Sara hopped over.

"Ben, come meet Nick, the new frog," said Sara. "He tells funny ☺ jokes." Nick was funny! Ben made a new frog friend.

In many stories, the character learns a lesson. Write words from the pond into the blanks to show the lesson Ben learned.

Ben was scared of something _____.

Ben learned that he could be _____ with

a _____ that was not the _____ as him.

same

friends   frog

new

SKILL Retell stories and demonstrate an understanding of their lesson

A PLAN FOR EMMA

On Monday, Emma tried basketball . She was not very good.

On Tuesday, Emma tried soccer . She was not very good.

On Wednesday, Emma tried to jump rope. She was not very good.

Her friend Kim was good at soccer.

"How did you get so good?" said Emma.

"I play soccer every day," said Kim. "You have to do something lots of times to get good at it."

Draw pictures to fill in the spaces on the calendar. On the first calendar, show what Emma did in the story. On the second calendar, show what Emma should do each day to get better at soccer. Hint: Think about what Kim suggested.

How Emma spent each day in the story:

MONDAY	TUESDAY	WEDNESDAY

A plan to help Emma to get better at soccer:

MONDAY	TUESDAY	WEDNESDAY

SKILL Retell stories and demonstrate an understanding of their lesson

SMALL MOUSE, BIG DAY

Min was a small mouse. He had a small scarf and a small hat.

Min liked small pieces of cheese . His mom gave him some

on a small plate.

"Thanks for the small snack!" said Min.

"Eat fast!" said his mom. "You have big things to do today!"

Circle the pictures of items that match the description of Min.

SKILL Describe characters, settings, and major events

MAKE THE MONSTER

Mog the Monster has five eyes . He has a funny nose. Mog the Monster has one big foot. He has funny hair. Mog the Monster has short arms. He has three ears .

Mog the Monster loves to ride his skateboard .

Draw a picture of Mog the Monster using the details in the story.

SKILL Describe characters, settings, and major events

SCRAMBLED SETTINGS

The setting is where the story happens. Draw a line to connect each mini story with a matching picture of the setting.

The bat's cave was dark and cool. The bat's cave had water and rocks in it.

Russ helped push the cart at the store. He pushed the cart by the eggs. Russ stopped by the milk.

"Look at the moon!" said Quinn. "This rocket will take us there fast!"

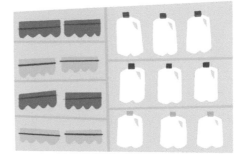

SKILL Describe characters, settings, and major events

GAME DAY

Ana liked playing soccer. It was game day for her team. Ana's team wore red. They ran fast. They kicked the ball hard. Dena kicked the ball to Ana. Ana kicked the ball into the goal!

"Go, Ana!" said Ana's dad.

Her team got four more goals and won!

Use the clues to complete the crossword puzzle.

1. Who kicked the ball to Ana?
2. What color did Ana's team wear?
3. Who cheered for Ana?
4. How many goals did Ana's team get **altogether**?

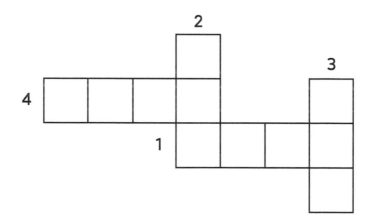

SKILL Describe the characters, settings, and major events

WHAT BIGS WANTS

Trey sat on the couch. His dog, Bigs, looked at him.

"Do you want some water?"

Bigs didn't want water.

"Do you want some food?"

Bigs didn't want food. Trey saw a ball on the floor. He picked it up. Bigs wagged his tail.

"Oh! You want to play with the ball!"

Underline the word(s) in the story that answer(s) each question. Use the colors indicated.

1. Who are the characters in this story?

2. Where was Trey sitting?

3. What things did Bigs NOT want?

4. What did Bigs do when Trey picked up the ball?

SKILL Describe the characters, settings, and major events

ALL ABOUT GRASSHOPPERS

Grasshoppers are insects. Grasshoppers use their mouths to eat. They eat plants. Grasshoppers use their legs to jump. They can jump very far. Grasshoppers use their color to hide. They can be green or brown. Grasshoppers use their wings to fly. They fly away to stay safe.

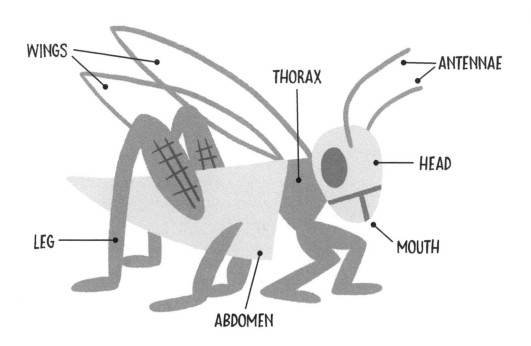

Mark each sentence below by coloring in the check if it's true or the X if it's false. Hint: Use information from both the words and the picture to help you.

1. Grasshoppers have four legs.

2. Their mouth is on their abdomen.

3. Grasshoppers eat plants.

4. Grasshoppers have two antennae.

SKILL Use illustrations and details to describe key ideas

APPLE TREE ALL YEAR

In the spring, you can see blooms on the apple tree. In the summer, you can see small apples on the apple tree. In the fall, you can see apples to pick on the apple tree. In the winter, you can see only branches on the apple tree.

Mark the picture according to the instructions below.

1. Circle what happens **after** blooms grow on the tree.
2. Draw an arrow to the season when apples are ready to pick.
3. Draw a box around what happens **before** the tree grows blooms.
4. Draw a happy face next to how the tree looks during your favorite season.

SKILL Use illustrations and details to describe key ideas

DRAW ALONG

You can draw a pig!

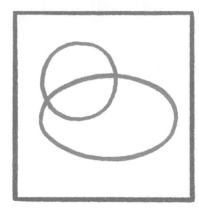  

1. First, draw a circle for the head and an oval for the body.

2. Then, draw rectangles for the legs and triangles for the ears.

3. Last, draw an oval for the nose. Add eyes, a mouth, and a tail.

Read the directions and use the pictures to draw your own pig. Use a pencil in case you want to erase anything. Give your pig a name.

SKILL Use illustrations and details to describe key ideas

ZOO TRIP

Welcome to the zoo! There are many fun things to do. You can see lots of animals.

Barn—Here you can see goats and chickens.

Big Cats—Here you can see lions and tigers.

Bug House—Here you can see spiders and worms.

Pond—Here you can see ducks and fish.

Fill in the blanks. Use the text and the map to help you.

1. The _____ is closest to the gate.

2. The big cats are far away from the _____.

3. Can you see giraffes at this zoo? _____

4. Can you see ducks at this zoo? _____

SKILL Use illustrations and details to describe key ideas

WHAT'S IN YOUR CUP?

At lunch, everyone picks a drink. Some kids have regular milk. Some kids have chocolate milk. Some kids have water. We made a chart to show the drinks everyone picked. The white cups are regular milk. The brown cups are chocolate milk. The blue cups are water.

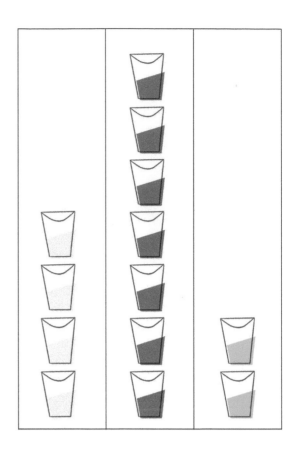

Circle the correct answer to fill in each blank. Use the chart above.

1. _____ kids had water.   [Five / Two]]

2. Most kids picked _____ milk.   [chocolate / regular]

3. The blue cups are _____.   [juice / water]

4. Four kids picked _____.   [water / regular milk]

SKILL Use illustrations and details to describe key ideas

ALL ABOUT PENGUINS

All penguins are birds. They cannot fly. All penguins have feathers. They are black and white. All penguins have beaks. They can eat fish. All penguins have flippers. They can swim in the ocean. All penguins hatch from eggs. The new penguins are called chicks.

Write one or two facts from the text in each blank space on the chart.

PENGUINS HAVE . . .	PENGUINS CAN . . .	PENGUINS CANNOT . . .

SKILL Ask and answer questions about key details

COUNTING BY FIVES

Counting by fives is fast. You can count many things by fives. You can count fingers by fives. I count my fingers like this: 5, 10. You can count toes by fives. I count my toes like this: 5, 10. You can count nickels by fives. I count nickels like this: 5, 10, 15, 20.

Write or draw three things from the text that you can count by fives in the blank spaces on the web.

Things to Count by Five

SKILL Ask and answer questions about key details

FROGS GROW UP

Frogs start as eggs. Next, tadpoles hatch from the eggs. The tadpoles have long tails. Next, they grow legs. Their legs get bigger and their tails get smaller. Soon, they are big frogs! Some of these frogs will lay eggs. What will happen next?

Write the numbers one through four on the lines beneath the pictures to put them in the order described in the text.

_____

_____

_____

_____

SKILL Ask and answer questions about key details

ANIMALS IN THE WINTER

In the winter, people stay warm inside. What about animals? In the winter, it is cold. That is why some birds fly away. In the winter, there is snow. That is why you can see animal tracks. In the winter, not much grows. That is why some animals hibernate.

Sometimes one thing makes another thing happen. This is called cause and effect. Draw a line from each cause to its effect.

Cause   **Effect**

LIFE IN A LOG CABIN

Long ago, some people lived in log cabins. Log cabins were small. Some had only one room. Log cabins had a big fireplace on one wall. The fireplace was for cooking. Log cabins had a bed and a table. There was not much room for other things. Log cabins had a door. Some had windows.

Use the details above to make a map of the things you would see in a log cabin.

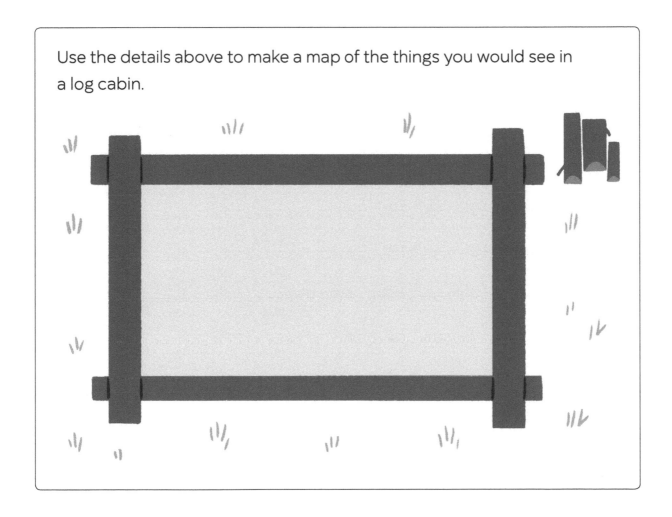

ALIVE IN THE YARD

There are many things living in my yard. Today I counted all the living things I saw. I looked in a tree and saw three **caterpillars**. I looked at the dirt and saw six **ants**. I looked on a bush and saw one **snail**. I made a chart of all the things I saw.

Use the text and the chart to answer the questions.

1. Which animal was seen the least? _____

2. How many ants were seen? _____

3. How many animals were seen in the tree? _____

4. Which animal was seen the most? _____

THE GREEN HILL NEIGHBORHOOD

The Green Hill neighborhood is a nice place to be. People can live in the homes there. People can play at the park there. People can shop at the stores there. People can learn at the school there. People can go to work there. People can do many things in the Green Hill neighborhood.

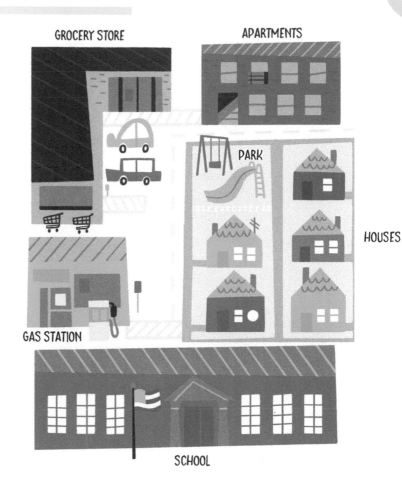

GROCERY STORE

APARTMENTS

PARK

HOUSES

GAS STATION

SCHOOL

1. Circle the places on the map where people could work.
2. Draw a line to show how to get from the apartments to the school.
3. Draw a box around a place to play.
4. Draw arrows to places where people can shop.

SKILL Use text features to locate key facts

WHERE WOULD YOU LOOK?

Table of Contents

You picked up a book called *All about California* to help your family plan a trip there. At the beginning is something called a table of contents. It shows what each section of the book is about and what page each section starts on. Answer each question by marking part of the table of contents in the color indicated.

Where would you look to find . . .

- how warm it is in California?   Yellow

- a map of how to get around California?   Green

- facts about the history of California?   Blue

- fun activities for your family in California?   Red

SKILL Use text features to locate key facts

OUTER SPACE

Earth is a planet floating in outer space. There are many things in outer space. The moon is in outer space. The stars are in outer space. Other planets are also in outer space. The sun is in outer space. Spaceships fly in outer space.

One of the planets in outer space is Saturn. It has rings.

Words that describe a picture are called a caption. Use the text and the caption to complete the crossword puzzle.

1. The planet in the picture is ____.
2. The planet in the picture has ____.
3. Something in space that starts with M.
4. Something in space that you see during the day.

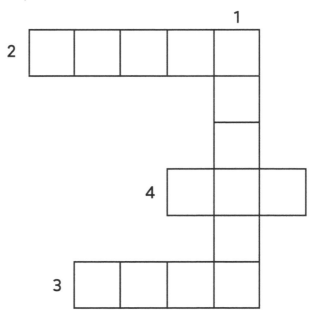

ALL ABOUT EYES

Eyes help people see things around them. The eyes have many parts. Eyelids help open and close the eye. Eyelashes help keep dirt out of the eye. The pupil and the iris let light into the eye. The iris can be many colors.

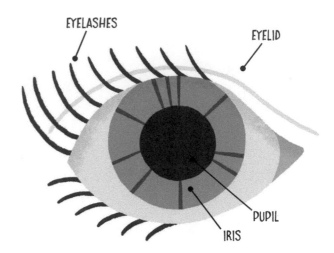

Make the following marks on the diagram:

1. Circle the part that keeps dirt out of the eye.
2. Put a check mark by the parts that let light into the eye.
3. Put an X by the part that opens and closes the eye.
4. Draw a box around the part that can be different colors.

SKILL Use text features to locate key facts

FROM WATER TO ICE

Before you read, it's helpful to think of what you already know about the topic. Then, you can connect new information to what you already know. This text is about ice. Using the checklist below, check off anything that you already know about ice.

☐ I have seen icicles.

☐ I have had ice cubes in a drink.

☐ I have stepped on ice.

☐ I have skated on ice.

When water gets very cold, it turns into ice. Water in a pond can turn into ice. Water dripping from a house can turn into ice. Water in the freezer can turn into ice. Water on the street can turn into ice. Be careful! Ice is slippery!

Underline anything from the passage that you haven't seen or heard of before.

SKILL Activate prior knowledge

LOOK! LADYBUGS!

Think of things that you already know about ladybugs. Write them on the chart below. After reading, see if there's anything new you learned that you can add to the chart.

	LADYBUGS HAVE ...	LADYBUGS CAN ...	LADYBUGS EAT ...
Before Reading			

	LADYBUGS HAVE ...	LADYBUGS CAN ...	LADYBUGS EAT ...
After Reading			

Ladybugs are insects. Ladybugs have wings. They can fly. Ladybugs have six legs. They can crawl on plants. Ladybugs have mouths. They can eat other insects or plants. Ladybugs have shells. They can be red, yellow, or orange. Some ladybugs have spots. They can have up to 24 spots.

SKILL Activate prior knowledge

ROCK AND ROLL

Mark the sentences "true" or "false" before reading. Color the check if you think the sentence is true. Color the X if you think the sentence is false. It's okay to guess if you don't know the answer. After reading, use what you learned to mark the sentences again. Did your thinking change?

	Before Reading	After Reading
1. Mountains are made of rock.	✓ ✗	✓ ✗
2. Sand is made of sugar.	✓ ✗	✓ ✗
3. Rocks cannot break.	✓ ✗	✓ ✗
4. Water can break rocks.	✓ ✗	✓ ✗

Some rocks are big and some are small. Mountains are made of big rocks. Sand is made of small rocks. Big rocks break into small rocks. Wind, water, heat, and cold can break big rocks. It takes a long time for a big rock to break into small rocks.

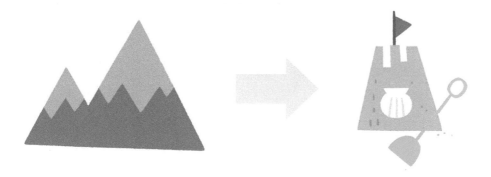

SKILL Activate prior knowledge

COMPUTERS EVERYWHERE

Computers are used for many things. Some computers are small. People use them to read and talk.

Some computers are in stores. People use them to sell and buy.

Some computers are at school. People use them to learn and have fun. How have you used computers?

Use the tip of a pencil to hold the end loop of a paper clip to the middle of the spinner. Flick the paper clip to spin it. Follow the instructions on the spinner to make connections between your life and the text. Spin it several times.

Tell about a store where you have seen a computer.

Have you used a computer? For what?

Have you seen someone else use a computer? For what?

Have you seen a computer at a school or library? What was it used for?

SKILL Make connections to self and the world

PIONEER KIDS

Long ago, many kids in the United States moved west with their families. They were called pioneers. The pioneer kids cooked food. They cooked over a fire. The pioneer kids liked to play. They played with toys made of wood. The pioneer kids had to go places. They went on foot or in wagons.

Compare your life to the life of a pioneer kid. Write similarities where the ovals overlap. Write differences in the outside part of the ovals.

Me   Pioneer Kid

SKILL Make connections to self and the world

LOST DOG!

Mateo went out to the mailbox. His dog, Lola, went too. Mateo looked at his mail. Mateo saw that Lola was not by him anymore. Oh no, Lola was lost! Mateo looked on the side of the house. He looked by the bushes.

What do you think will happen next? Write your prediction in the space. Then keep reading.

I predict _____   Check your prediction:

_____   ✓ ✗

_____.

If your prediction was right, color in the check mark. If you had to change your thinking, color in the X. It's okay to change your thinking. Good readers do it all the time.

He heard a bark and looked up. Lola was looking out the window of the house. She had already gone inside!

SKILL Answer questions about key details

SNEAKING STRAWBERRIES

Wes helped his mom pick a bowl of strawberries to make jam. On the walk back, he ate a few. While his mom washed her hands, Wes ate a few more. While his mom got a spoon, Wes ate a few more.

"What happened to the strawberries?" asked Wes's mom.

Wes smiled. "Oh well, there are a few left to put on top of yogurt."

Complete the crossword puzzle.

1. When asked about the strawberries, Wes _____.

2. Who ate most of the strawberries? _____

3. The characters are Wes and his _____.

4. The strawberries were collected in a _____.

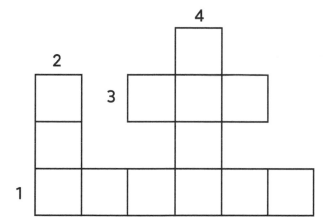

SKILL Answer questions about key details

TRINA'S RABBIT

Sometimes an author doesn't explain exactly what happened in a story. You have to use what you already know, along with clues the author gives, to figure it out. This is called making an inference. Read each section of the story. Then color the smiley face next to the inference that matches the clues the author gave.

STORY		INFERENCES
Trina always had her toy rabbit with her. She took it shopping. She took it outside.	☺ ☺	The rabbit is Trina's favorite toy. Trina doesn't like the rabbit very much.
Trina's grandma said, "Can I wash your rabbit?"	☺ ☺	Trina's grandma is mean. The rabbit is getting dirty.
"No!" said Trina. "Don't take him!" When Trina took a nap, her grandma took the rabbit. She put it back before Trina woke up. When Trina woke up, she said, "My rabbit smells so fresh!"	☺ ☺	Grandma played with the rabbit while Trina was asleep. Grandma washed the rabbit while Trina was asleep.

SKILL Answer questions about key details

THE SNAIL AND THE ANT

A snail and an ant wanted to race.

"I am faster than a snail! I will win!" said the ant. The race started. The ant ran fast! The snail slid along slowly. The ant stopped to have a snack. Then he felt tired.

"I'll take a quick nap," said the ant. The snail kept going. When the ant woke up, the snail had won the race!

Answer each question by circling the correct picture.

1. Which animal can move the fastest?

2. Which animal took a break during the race?

3. Which animal won the race?

4. Which animal showed what can happen when you work hard and never give up?

DRESSING UP

I like to play dress up. I dress up in boots and a shirt. Then I can play farm. I dress up in a cape and a mask. Then I can play superhero. I dress up in a hat and wings. Then I can play zoo. I can be many different things!

Make the following marks on the picture:

1. Circle the item that can be used with a cape to play superhero.
2. Draw a box around the items needed to play farm.
3. Draw an arrow to the items needed to play zoo.
4. Draw a smiley face next to your favorite dress-up item.

SKILL Answer questions about key details

TREE TROUBLES

Leo was flying a kite. The wind pulled his kite into a tree! Leo didn't know how to get it down.

"I can help!" said Lisa. Lisa went up in the tree and pushed the branch down.

"I still can't reach it!" said Leo.

"I can help!" said Marcos. Marcos got a step for Leo to stand on.

"I got it! Thanks for your help!" said Leo.

Draw what happened in the middle of the story.

SKILL Retell stories and demonstrate an understanding of their lesson

A FUN WAY TO PLAY

Mya was building with blocks.

"Can I play, too?" asked Tim.

"No," said Mya. "You will mess up my tower."

"Can I play blocks?" asked Chun.

"No," said Mya. "I want to do it myself."

Soon, Mya had no more ideas for the blocks.

"Can we make a bridge?" asked Rena.

"Sure!" said Mya. "Great idea!"

Fill in the blank to show what Mya learned in this story.

At first, I didn't want to let anyone else play.
But then I learned that

_____

_____

_____.

SKILL Retell stories and demonstrate an understanding of their lesson

THE BIG SHOW

It was time for Cora's dance show to start.

"You will be great!" said her dance teacher. Cora felt hot.

"You can do it!" said her dance teacher. Cora felt sick.

"I can help you calm down," said the teacher. "Take two big breaths, then dance." Cora took two breaths and felt a little better. She danced her best!

Write the numbers one through four on the lines beneath the pictures to put them in the order described in the text.

_____

_____

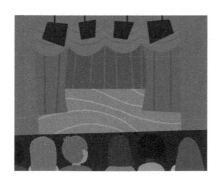

_____

_____

SKILL Retell stories and demonstrate an understanding of their lesson

KITCHEN BAND

My brother came into the kitchen. He found a bowl and patted it with his hands. My sister came into the kitchen. She found a pan and hit it with a fork. I came into the kitchen. I found two spoons and tapped them. Dad came into the kitchen.

"What is going on?" he said. "I was taking a nap."

Write the numbers one to four next to the characters to show the order they came into the story.

SKILL Retell stories and demonstrate an understanding of their lesson

MORNING SURPRISE

My grandpa said, "Time to get up."

I hate getting up early! I got dressed and ate. I hate getting up early! I brushed my teeth. I hate getting up early!

"Look outside!" said Grandpa. There were deer on the lawn. "They only come out when it's early," he said.

What a great surprise!

Mark each sentence below by coloring in the check if it's true, or the X if it's false.

1. The boy learned that he could find something good, even at a time of day he didn't like.

2. In the beginning, the boy was just waking up.

3. In the middle, the boy went to school.

4. In the end, the boy was still grouchy.

SKILL Retell stories and demonstrate an understanding of their lesson

INSIDE ADVENTURES

Fox lived in a den under a tree. One day, it snowed. Fox's friend, Bear, came to visit. They had to stay inside. They drew pictures at the table. They played cards on the rug. They ate berries by the fireplace. Fox and Bear were very busy inside.

Draw the story's setting below using clues from the text.

SKILL Describe characters, settings, and major events

HOW MANNY PLAYS

Manny plays football with his team every Saturday. In football, you have to run. Manny runs as fast as he can. In football, you have to help. Manny helps his team. In football, you have to be a good sport.

Manny says, "Good game!" to the other team.

Find an example in the story that proves each sentence below and underline it with the indicated color.

1. Manny is a good teammate. *Red*

2. Manny is active. *Green*

3. Manny is kind. *Yellow*

4. Manny tries his best. *Blue*

SKILL Describe characters, settings, and major events

THE WAITING GAME

Allie was waiting to get a haircut. She hated waiting!

"Let's play a game while we wait," said Allie's mom. "Can you find something red?" Allie saw a red coat.

"Find something blue," said Allie's mom. Allie saw a blue chair.

"Find something yellow," said Allie's mom. Allie saw a yellow sign. Then, Allie's name was called! It was her turn.

Complete the sentences below to tell about the problem and solution in this story.

Problem	**Solution**
The problem is that Allie	To help make the waiting easier, Allie's mom
_____	_____
_____	_____
_____ .	_____ .

SKILL Describe characters, settings, and major events

BASKETBALL FRIENDS

Kevin and Zack always played basketball together. One day, Kevin saw Zack playing with someone else. Kevin felt sad. He sat by himself. The basketball rolled over. Zack ran to get it.

"Oh, there you are," said Zack. "Come meet Gio. We can all play together."

Kevin was happy. Zack still wanted to play with him and the new friend!

KEVIN
☐ ☐ ☐

GIO
☐ ☐ ☐

ZACK
☐ ☐ ☐

Put a check by:
- the character who runs into a problem in the story.
- the character whose feelings we know the most about.
- the character whose feelings change.

The character with the most check marks is the main character.

SKILL Describe characters, settings, and major events

LITTLE SQUIRREL'S WORK

No one saw the squirrel who picked up acorns at the park. Visitors liked the ducks but never saw Little Squirrel. This made her sad, so she stayed in her tree all day and did nothing. The next day a runner tripped on an acorn. Oh no! Little Squirrel had work to do! She smiled. Even if no one saw her, she was needed in the park.

Sometimes authors share their message by showing how a character changes. Circle the words that describe how Little Squirrel felt at the beginning of the story and at the end. Talk about what made her feelings change.

Beginning

happy

excited

sad

tired

unimportant

End

helpful

sad

important

needed

hungry

SKILL Describe characters, settings, and major events

MOVIE NIGHT

It's Friday night!

Let's get ready!

Pop! Pop! Pop!

The popcorn is made.

Click! I turn off the lights,

The room is dark.

Squish! We sit together,

A fuzzy blanket around us.

Tap, tap, tap.

The movie turns on.

Shhhhhh!

Let's watch!

Underline parts of the poem to match the key below:

Mark things you can imagine hearing in red.

Mark things you can imagine feeling in blue.

Mark things you can imagine seeing in green.

SKILL Identify feeling and sensory words

MY PET CAT

Before reading, write words that fit each description. Then transfer them to the matching numbered lines below. Read the silly story with the sensory words you came up with.

1. a word that describes a smell _____

2. a color _____

3. a word that describes a sound _____

I have a pet cat.

My sister says, "Why does the cat smell

so _____?" That's just the way he is.
1

My mom says, "Why does the cat look

so _____?" That's just the way he is.
2

My brother says, "Why does the cat sound

so _____?" That's just the way he is.
3

There is no other cat like him!

SKILL Identify feeling and sensory words

AT THE AIRPORT

As you read, stop and decide what feeling each section suggests. Color the happy face next to the feeling that makes the most sense.

STORY		RYAN FEELS
Ryan was picking up his grandpa at the airport. "There are so many people here," said Ryan. "I don't want to get lost!"	🙂	Calm
	🙂	Scared
Grandpa's plane was late. "This is taking a long time," said Ryan. "There is nothing to do!"	🙂	Bored
	🙂	Happy
Ryan looked out the window. "Grandpa's plane is coming this way!" said Ryan. "I can't wait to give him a hug!"	🙂	Excited
	🙂	Tired

SKILL Identify feeling and sensory words

WHAT AM I?

Read each riddle. Use the sensory clues to figure out what the riddle is describing. Draw a line from the riddle to the item being described.

I am soft and fluffy. Use me when you are sleepy.

I am sweet and colorful. You can find me at a party.

I am round, smooth, and hard. Kids have fun with me outside.

I am cold and wet. You can only find me in the winter.

I am small and soft. You can hear my song.

SKILL Identify feeling and sensory words

AT THE BUS STOP

The street is quiet,
Except for kids,
And birds,
Chattering.
In the fresh, cool air,
I zip my coat.
Yellow lights blink,
At the end of the street.
Chhhh! The bus stops,
The door clanks open,
And we stomp up the stairs.
We're on our way to school!

In the boxes below, write things from the text that you can imagine seeing, hearing, or feeling.

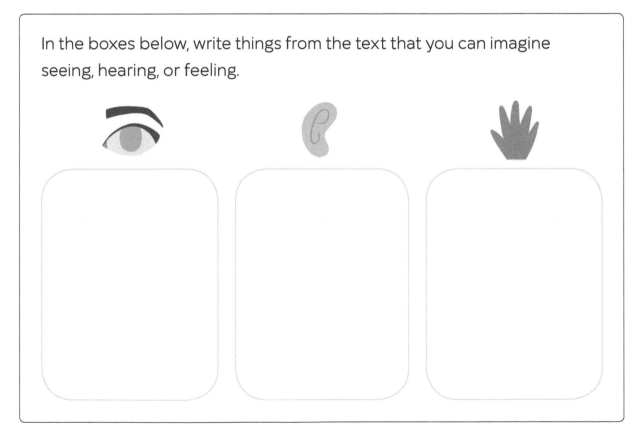

SKILL Identify feeling and sensory words

DON'T COPY ME!

Logan and Pablo were painting.

"I like green!" said Logan.

"Me, too!" said Pablo.

"Don't copy me!" said Logan. "I like painting animals."

"Me, too!" said Pablo.

"Don't copy me!" said Logan.

The boys shared their pictures. Logan painted a green fish. Pablo painted a green bird. Pablo did not copy Logan!

Complete the crossword below about the characters' similarities.

1. Both characters are _____.
2. What activity are both characters doing in the story?
3. Both characters like to paint _____.
4. Both characters like the color _____.

SKILL Compare and contrast the experiences of characters

MAKING PIZZA

Keesha and Rita were making pizzas. Both girls put sauce on their pizza. Both girls put cheese on their pizza. Both girls put meat on their pizza. Keesha put on pepperoni and Rita put on sausage. Both girls put vegetables on their pizza. Keesha put on mushrooms and Rita put on peppers. The pizzas were tasty!

Draw the correct toppings on each girl's pizza.

Keesha's Pizza   Rita's Pizza

SKILL Compare and contrast the experiences of characters

THE PRIZE DRAWING

Mrs. West's class had been earning "good job" tickets. Omar got a ticket for cleaning up the room. Shelby got a ticket for holding the door for others. Soon, Mrs. West's jar was full of tickets the kids had earned. She pulled out one ticket.

"Omar, it's your ticket! You win a prize!" said Mrs. West. Omar cheered. Shelby frowned.

Imagine what Omar and Shelby would say about the ticket drawing if you talked to them. Use clues from the text to fill in the blanks.

Omar

I felt _____

because _____

_____

_____.

Shelby

I felt _____

because _____

_____

_____.

SKILL Compare and contrast the experiences of characters

NEIGHBORS AND FRIENDS

Faith and Mrs. Conway live on the same street. Mrs. Conway is older and Faith is younger. The two neighbors like sharing stories on the porch. Faith shares about school. Mrs. Conway shares about her grandkids. The neighbors work in the garden together. Faith pulls weeds and Mrs. Conway waters the plants. They are good friends!

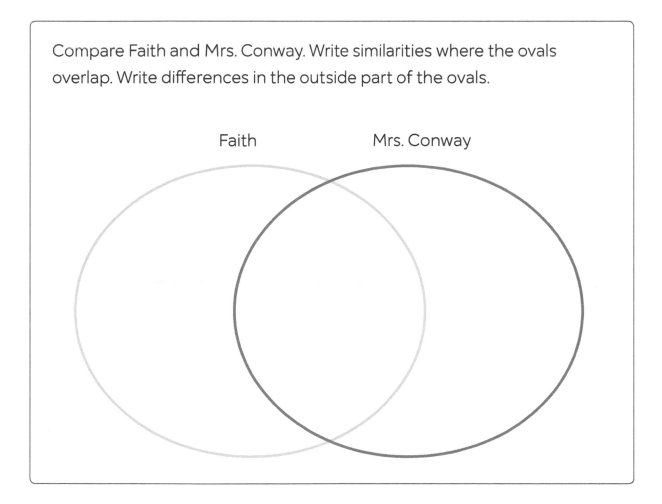

Compare Faith and Mrs. Conway. Write similarities where the ovals overlap. Write differences in the outside part of the ovals.

Faith   Mrs. Conway

SKILL Compare and contrast the experiences of characters

HOW TO CARVE A PUMPKIN

It's fun to carve a pumpkin in fall. An adult can help you. First, cut the top off the pumpkin with a knife. Next, scoop out the insides with a spoon. After that, draw a face on the pumpkin with a marker. Then, cut out the face with a knife. Last, put a light in the pumpkin. Now your pumpkin is done!

Start at the star. Color the arrows to make a path showing the steps in order. Hint: Many steps only show the tool that is used.

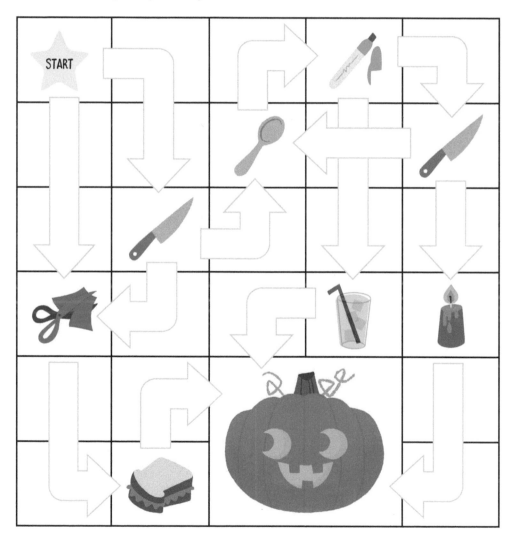

SKILL Ask and answer questions about key details

CITY ANIMALS

Some animals live in cities. Mice can live in cities. They eat food that people throw away. Squirrels can also live in cities. They live in trees. Raccoons can live in cities. They take food from trash cans. Sometimes raccoons live in trees. Dogs also live in cities. They live inside because they are not wild animals.

Circle pictures of animals that match each statement.

1. Animals that live in the city

2. Animal that is not wild

3. Animals that can live in trees

4. Animals that eat people's trash

SKILL Ask and answer questions about key details

NEEDS AND WANTS

People can choose to spend money on many things. People spend money on things they have to have to stay alive. These things are called needs. Food, clothes, and shelter are needs. People also spend money on things that are fun. These things are called wants. Games, candy, and toys are wants.

Write three needs and three wants from the passage into the chart below.

NEEDS	WANTS

Talk about some things that you need and want.

_____

_____

TAKING CARE OF A CACTUS

A cactus is a plant. It can live indoors if you take care of it. A cactus needs only a little bit of water. You can water it one time per week. During the winter, you can stop watering the cactus. A cactus needs lots of sun. Put it near a window. Enjoy your indoor cactus!

Mark each sentence below by coloring in the check if it's true, or the X if it's false.

1. A cactus needs water every day. ✓ ✗

2. You can stop watering a cactus in the winter. ✓ ✗

3. A cactus needs a lot of sun. ✓ ✗

4. A cactus has to live outside. ✓ ✗

SKILL Ask and answer questions about key details

ALL ABOUT FOSSILS

Fossils are made when something living dies and is covered up with dirt. After a long time, some of these covered things turn into stone. Sometimes animal bones turn into fossils. Sometimes plants turn into fossils. Fossils give us clues about the plants and animals that lived long ago.

Complete the crossword below about fossils.

1. To become a fossil, something that died has to be _____ in dirt.
2. When a fossil forms, the dead thing is turned to _____.
3. It takes a _____ time for a fossil to form.
4. Animal _____ can become fossils.

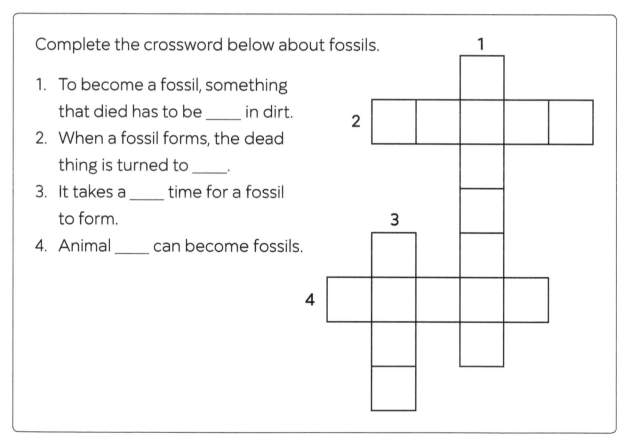

FUN IN THE DIRT

Dirt bikes have two wheels. They come in many different sizes. Kids can learn to ride on smaller dirt bikes. Dirt bikes are for riding on dirt trails, not on streets. To be safe, you should wear a helmet, jacket, and gloves when riding a dirt bike. People who like to race can take their dirt bike on a dirt track. Many people enjoy riding dirt bikes.

Underline the following topics in the color indicated each time you see them in the passage:

helmets  Blue

dirt bikes Yellow

racing Green

dirt tracks Red

Which topic was underlined the most? This is the main topic.

SKILL Identify the main topic and retell key details

AMERICA'S PASTIME

Many people like to play and watch baseball. Baseball is played on a diamond-shaped field. The field has four bases. Players from one team take turns trying to hit the ball. When a player runs around all four bases, they get a point. Nine players from the other team play in the field. They try to catch the ball.

Which topic is mentioned the most in the reading passage? Write this topic on the web where it says "Main Topic." Use facts from the text to fill in the blanks in the details.

Main Topic:

_____

_____ players from one team play in the field.

One team tries to hit the ball. The other team tries to _____ the ball.

The field is _____-shaped.

SKILL Identify the main topic and retell key details

FIREFIGHTERS WORKING

The main topic of the text below is firefighters. Read each detail. If the detail tells us more about firefighters, color the check. This is a detail to remember. If the detail doesn't tell us more about firefighters, color the X. These details are less important.

DETAIL	Does this detail tell us more about the topic (firefighters)?	
Fire is dangerous.	✓	✗
Firefighters do many things to help us stay safe from fire.	✓	✗
Firefighters teach kids what to do if there is a fire.	✓	✗
Fire can burn skin.	✓	✗
Firefighters wear special clothes to keep them safe from fire.	✓	✗
Water can help put out a fire.	✓	✗
Firefighters use hoses, axes, and ladders to put fires out.	✓	✗

SKILL Identify the main topic and retell key details

ANTS ALL AROUND

Ants are all around us. Ants build nests under or on top of the ground. People don't like bugs in their homes, but sometimes ants get inside. Ants have six legs. They have jaws to tear apart food. Ants are strong. They can carry food back to their nests. Sweep up your crumbs or ants will find them!

Some details are more important than others. For each detail below, color the star if it tells us something important about ants. Color the minus sign if the detail doesn't tell us something important about ants.

1. People don't like bugs in their homes. ☆ ▭	2. Ants build nests. ☆ ▭
3. Ants have jaws. ☆ ▭	4. Sweep up your crumbs. ☆ ▭

SKILL Identify the main topic and retell key details

THE DESERT

Deserts may be hot or cold. They are always dry. Deserts do not get much rain.

Some animals can live in deserts. Lizards, rats, and foxes are all desert animals.

It is hard for things to grow in the desert. Bushes and grasses that don't need much water live in the desert. Cacti also live in the desert.

Longer texts are sometimes divided into sections. Authors use headings to show what each section is mostly about. Write each heading into the blank space where it makes the most sense. Hint: The heading should match all the details in the section it belongs to.

Plants

Weather

Wildlife

SKILL Use text features to locate key facts

OCEAN INDEX

Index

beaches, 15, 26

depth, 13

fish, 20

hurricanes, 31

ocean floor, 3, 9

ocean travel, 12

Pacific Ocean, 6, 17, 30

saltwater, 4

sharks, 7, 29

size, 4

tide pools, 19

whales, 30

Some books have an index. Indexes are found at the back of a book and show what page to look at for specific topics. Some topics can be found on more than one page. The index above is from a book about oceans. Answer each question below by writing in the correct page number(s).

1. Where would you look for information about sharks? _____

2. What page tells about hurricanes? _____

3. Where would you look to find out about the size of oceans? _____

4. If you didn't know what a tide pool was, where could you find out? _____

VOLCANOES

Inside of the Earth there is hot **magma**. Magma pushes up through the Earth's **crust**. This is a volcano! The magma cools and makes new rocks. Sometimes, ash **erupts** from a volcano instead of magma. Sometimes when a volcano erupts, it causes a **landslide**. Volcanoes can be dangerous.

Glossary

crust: the outside layer of rocks on the Earth

erupt: to shoot out or explode

landslide: when dirt and rocks slide down from a mountain or cliff

magma: hot, liquid rock, also called lava

A glossary tells the meaning of the bold words in the text. Use clues from the text and the glossary to write each of the four glossary words in the correct place on the diagram.

SKILL Use text features to locate key facts

THE WESTWOOD LIBRARIES WEBSITE

Welcome to the
Westwood Libraries

My Account	About	Search	Contact us
	Hours		
	Locations		
	Homework Help		
	My Special Events		
	Library Staff		

Websites are organized using menus. Sometimes, when you touch a word on a menu with your cursor, more choices drop down. The menu shown above is from a website about a group of libraries. Circle words on the menu in the colors indicated to show where you would click to find the following information:

- When the libraries are open   *Yellow*

- Where to find the closest library   *Blue*

- How to get help with your homework   *Red*

- How to call the library   *Green*

SKILL Use text features to locate key facts

BUTTERFLY BASICS

Butterflies and Their Food

Butterflies eat a sweet liquid from flowers called nectar. Butterflies get the nectar using a long tube on their head. It works like a straw.

Butterfly Life Cycle

Butterflies change during their lives. They start as an egg. When they hatch, they are caterpillars. Next, they turn into a chrysalis. Finally, a butterfly comes out of the chrysalis!

For each passage, check off the things you noticed. Talk about what is the same or different about the two passages.

	Butterflies and Their Food	Butterfly Life Cycle
TOPIC	☐ Flowers ☐ Butterflies	☐ Flowers ☐ Butterflies
FACTS	☐ How butterflies eat ☐ How butterflies change	☐ How butterflies eat ☐ How butterflies change
PICTURES	☐ Shows one thing a butterfly does ☐ Shows how a butterfly changes	☐ Shows one thing a butterfly does ☐ Shows how a butterfly changes

SKILL Compare and contrast two texts on the same topic

COLORFUL COLORADO

Things to Do in Colorado

There are many fun things to do in Colorado. You can go camping or skiing in the Rocky Mountains. It's fun to visit the zoo. You can go to a football game.

Colorado's Mountains

Colorado has very tall mountains. They are called the Rocky Mountains. It is very cold at the top of the mountains. Animals like deer and bighorn sheep live in the Rocky Mountains.

Color-code the two passages according to the directions below.

Circle one or more words in each passage that show the topic.

Underline something that is mentioned in both passages. Mark it in both passages.

Underline a fact in each passage that is unique (not mentioned in the other passage).

SKILL Compare and contrast two texts on the same topic

A LOOK AT BONES

Bones Protect

Bones protect soft parts of your body. Your skull protects your brain. Your ribs protect your heart and lungs. Parts of your body could get crushed without bones.

What Bones Do

Bones give your body shape. Leg bones help hold you up so you can walk. Without bones, your body would be a blob on the floor.

Write the words from each rectangle onto the correct part of the diagram. The overlapping part of the ovals is for words that describe both passages.

Bones give us shape.	Skulls protect brains.	Topic: bones

Bones Protect   **What Bones Do**

SKILL Compare and contrast two texts on the same topic

ART PARTNERS

Beth was a great artist but also very messy. Jason liked to keep things neat. Sometimes they didn't get along because they were so different.

"My picture is missing something but I don't know what," said Jason.

"You need a snowman right here," said Beth. "I can't finish because I need a blue marker."

"I put the marker over here with the other ones," said Jason. They both finished great work!

Write questions that someone could answer after reading the text.

The answer is *Beth.* What is the question?

Who _____

_____ ?

The answer is *blue.* What is the question?

What _____

_____ ?

THE CAR TRACK

Henry was looking at a car track at the store.

"I've got to have this!" said Henry.

"No, it costs a lot of money," said Henry's mom.

Later at home, Henry saw his box of chalk in the closet. He got an idea. Henry took the chalk outside and drew curves and lines on the driveway. He brought out his toy cars.

"What are you up to?" asked Henry's mom.

"I made my own car track!" said Henry.

Complete the crossword below.

1. The track at the store was too much ____.
2. Henry drew on the ____.
3. He drew curves and ____.
4. Henry drew with ____.

OH, SNOW!

Emma got a skateboard for her birthday. She worked hard to learn how to ride it. The best part about riding her skateboard was going fast! One day, Emma woke up to see the ground covered in snow. "How will I ride my skateboard now?" she wondered. Emma's dad could see that she was sad.

"Hey, Emma!" he said. "Let's find my old sled in the garage." Soon, Emma was going fast again, this time down hills of snow.

Mark each sentence below by coloring in the check if it's true, or the X if it's false.

1. Emma is afraid of going fast.

2. There are two characters in this story.

3. Emma couldn't ride her skateboard because of the rain.

4. The sled belongs to Emma's dad.

SKILL Answer questions about key details

ROSY'S ESCAPE

Rosy the parrot was tired of eating birdseed. If only she could open the door to her cage, she would get the cookie on the table! Rosy sat on her perch to think about how to get out. The perch tilted a little to the side. The bar was loose! Rosy pulled the wooden bar out of her perch. Holding it in her beak, she pushed the latch open. Rosy enjoyed a cookie feast!

Draw lines from each question to the picture that shows the answer.

1. Who is the main character?

2. What did the character want?

3. What stopped the character from getting what she wanted?

4. What did the character use to solve the problem?

SKILL Answer questions about key details

THE EMPTY POT

Long ago in China, the emperor had to choose who would be the next emperor.

He said, "Each child will get a seed. After one year, bring me your pots."

Chen planted and watered his seed. After a year, nothing grew. All the other children had beautiful flowers.

The emperor said, "The seeds I gave out were bad. The children who grew flowers must have cheated. Chen, you will be the new emperor because you are honest."

Use the tip of a pencil to hold the end loop of a paper clip to the middle of the spinner. Flick the paper clip to spin it. Follow the instructions on the spinner to tell something about the story out loud. Spin it several times.

Tell about the . . .

middle

beginning

end

lesson

characters

setting

SKILL Retell stories and demonstrate an understanding of their lesson

A PAPER GIFT

Dante wanted to give his mom a nice Christmas gift, but he didn't have any money. At school, Dante noticed his friend doing something with paper.

"What are you working on, Emily?" he asked.

"I'm folding this paper to make a bird called a crane," she said. Emily showed Dante how to do it, too.

On Christmas morning, Dante's mom opened her gift. It was five paper cranes strung together. Dante's mom loved it!

The "somebody, wanted, but, so" model is a good way to retell a story. Use words or pictures to complete each part of the model. Can you retell the four parts you identified?

Somebody . . . (the main character)	Wanted . . . (the character's goal)	But . . . (the problem that got in the character's way)	So . . . (how the problem was solved)

SKILL Retell stories and demonstrate an understanding of their lesson

THE BOOK REPORT

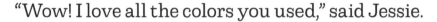

Alex was making a poster about a book. He wrote the title on top, drew a picture, and glued on his book report. Alex stepped back and frowned. Some of his letters were not the same size and he had colored outside of the lines a little bit.

Alex took the poster to school, feeling sad because it wasn't perfect.

"Wow! I love all the colors you used," said Jessie.

"You're so good at drawing people," said Dylan.

Alex smiled. No one even noticed his small mistakes.

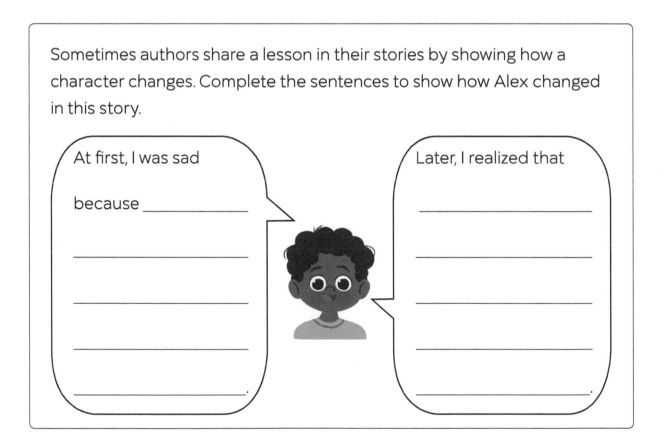

Sometimes authors share a lesson in their stories by showing how a character changes. Complete the sentences to show how Alex changed in this story.

At first, I was sad

because _____

_____

_____

_____

Later, I realized that

_____

_____

_____

_____

SKILL Retell stories and demonstrate an understanding of their lesson

TOOTH TROUBLE

Penny had her first loose tooth.

Her dad said, "I'll pull it out for you."

"No!" said Penny, "I'm afraid it will hurt."

"Just pull hard!" said her brother.

Penny was too scared to pull on it.

At dinner, Penny said, "This tooth is never going to come out!"

She took a bite out of an apple. She was about to take another bite when she saw her loose tooth stuck in the apple! She hadn't even noticed that it came out.

"That wasn't so bad!" she said.

Use the "somebody, wanted, but, so" model to retell this story. The square in the upper left corner represents "somebody." Start there. Then color the arrows to move through the correct "wanted," "but," and "so" pictures.

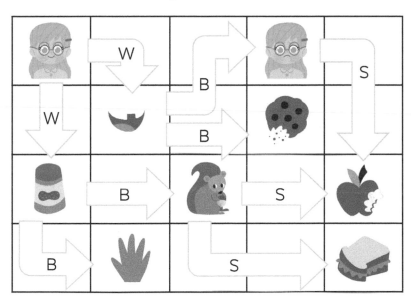

W = Wanted
B = But
S = So

A TOUGH CHOICE

Liam got an invitation to his friend Mario's birthday party on Saturday!

"Hmm," said Liam's mom. "You have baseball on Saturday. You'll have to choose one activity or the other."

Liam had a hard choice to make.

On Saturday morning, Liam's mom asked, "What have you decided to do today?"

"I'm going to the party," he said. "Danny has wanted to play third base for a while so today will be his chance. It's important to me to be with my friend Mario today."

Sometimes the problem in a story is happening inside a character's mind. Circle the best answers below to tell about Liam's problem.

I wanted to go to the party and the _____.

game   store   park

It was _____ to make the choice.

easy   fun   hard

I picked the _____ because it was important to _____.

game   get exercise
park   be with Mario
party   save money

SKILL Describe characters, settings, and major events

THE COLOR HUNT

"I'm so bored," I said.

"Try this," said Dad. "Find one thing that is each color in the rainbow and put it in this bag."

I looked all around our apartment. I found a red car, an orange brush, a yellow teddy bear, a green crayon, and a blue glove. I looked and looked but couldn't find anything purple. Then I got an idea.

"I'm done!" I said.

"Why is your hand in the bag?" asked Dad.

"Because my nail polish is purple!" I said.

Draw a picture or write words to show the characters, setting, problem, and solution.

Characters	Setting

Problem	Solution

SKILL Describe characters, settings, and major events

THE MAGIC FLOWERPOT

Edna the Fairy had a magic flowerpot.

Edna said, "Magic pot, grow me a rose." A plant sprang up from the pot. Edna clapped twice and it stopped growing. When Edna went out, her friend Lily wanted to try.

Lily said, "Magic pot, grow me a grapevine." A vine grew out of the pot. It got bigger and bigger. Lily couldn't make it stop! Edna flew in and clapped twice.

"Thank you!" said Lily. "The vine was almost growing out the window."

Sometimes one action makes something else happen. This is called cause and effect. Write or draw a picture to fill in each missing cause or effect.

CAUSE	EFFECT
Magic pot, grow me a rose.	
	Rose stops growing.

SKILL Describe characters, settings, and major events

GOING TO ALIEN SCHOOL

Zeep was an alien who lived on Mars. He was about to start alien school and his dad was showing him how to walk there.

"First, you walk to the big red rock," said his dad. "Then you go past two craters."

"One, two," Zeep said as they walked by.

"Next, look for the red sandpit," said Zeep's dad. "When you get there, turn left."

"Oh, I see the school!" said Zeep. "It's just up ahead!"

Design a postcard to match the setting of this story. Write the name of the place and draw what it looks like.

SKILL Describe characters, settings, and major events

THE GRUMPY GOAT

A grumpy goat lived under a bridge. He wouldn't let anyone cross. One day, a boy came along.

He said, "Goat, I'll give you a carrot if you let me cross."

"No way!" said the goat.

"How about a new scarf?"

"No!" said the goat.

"Let's cross together, and I'll take you with me to the fair," said the boy.

"Really?" said the goat. "I got lost on the way to the fair last year, and I've been under this bridge ever since. Let's go!"

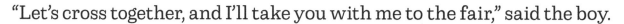

Read the two lists below. Check off the parts you see in this text. The list with the most checks tells the type of text (fiction or nonfiction).

STORY (FICTION)	
	characters
	a setting
	a problem and solution
	something make believe

INFORMATION (NONFICTION)	
	about real things
	facts
	explains something
	text features (headings, index, captions, etc.)

SKILL Explain the difference between fiction and nonfiction

THE TRUTH ABOUT GOATS

Habitat

Goats live all over the world. They can be found in the wild and on farms. Wild goats sometimes live high up in the mountains.

Uses

People use goats for milk, for meat, for their hair, and to pull carts. A goat's hair is used to make carpets and clothes.

Food

Goats are plant eaters. They like grasses and hay. Goats have four stomachs to break down their food.

Read the two lists below. Check off the parts you see in this text. The list with the most checks tells the type of text (fiction or nonfiction).

STORY (FICTION)	
	characters
	a setting
	a problem and solution
	something make believe

INFORMATION (NONFICTION)	
	about real things
	facts
	explains something
	text features (headings, index, captions, etc.)

SKILL Explain the difference between fiction and nonfiction

WHICH TYPE OF TEXT?

In each pair of sentences, one is from a story text (fiction) and the other is from an informational text (nonfiction). Circle one of the words next to each sentence to show which sentence is which.

The dragon said, "I hate having bananas for dinner."	STORY (FICTION)	INFORMATIONAL (NONFICTION)
Bananas are a kind of fruit.	STORY (FICTION)	INFORMATIONAL (NONFICTION)

Fish and frogs live in a lake habitat.	STORY (FICTION)	INFORMATIONAL (NONFICTION)
Once there was a girl who lived by a lake.	STORY (FICTION)	INFORMATIONAL (NONFICTION)

Someone broke Baby Bear's chair!	STORY (FICTION)	INFORMATIONAL (NONFICTION)
Bears can eat meat and some plants.	STORY (FICTION)	INFORMATIONAL (NONFICTION)

Hockey is a sport played on ice.	STORY (FICTION)	INFORMATIONAL (NONFICTION)
Hazel's team won their hockey game!	STORY (FICTION)	INFORMATIONAL (NONFICTION)

SKILL Explain the difference between fiction and nonfiction

THE AWARD GOES TO . . .

Fiction and nonfiction texts are used for different reasons. Draw a line from each award to the text that deserves it most.

How to Paint a Room

First, cover the floor with drop cloths. Then, use a brush to paint around the doors, windows, and trim. Last, use a paint roller to paint the largest parts of the wall.

The Paint Monster

While painting a picture, I got some paint on my fingers. I scratched my nose and brushed my hair out of my face. I touched my chin.

Mom said, "You look like a paint monster!" I looked in a mirror. Every part of my face I had touched had paint on it!

SILLIEST

TEACHES SOMETHING

TRUE INFORMATION

TELLS A STORY

SKILL Explain the difference between fiction and nonfiction

SIDEWALK SCARE

This is the same story told by two different characters. Draw a picture of the character that is telling each version.

I was out walking on a rainy day. Then I saw something long and pink by my foot. It was a worm! I almost stepped on it! I picked it up and put it back in the dirt.

I was out on a rainy day. Boom! A big foot hit the ground next to me! I was almost smashed! Then I was lifted up high and set down in the dirt. I was lucky to be alive!

SKILL Identify who is telling the story

BEING SMALL

Mason didn't like being small. He was too small for his brother Justin's football team.

One day Justin said, "Come play hide-and-seek with me."

"Sure!" said Mason.

Justin counted, "One, two, three . . ."

When he got to ten, he went to find Mason. He couldn't find Mason.

Justin said, "I give up! Where are you?"

"I'm right here!" said Mason as he came out from behind a couch.

"I didn't think anyone could fit back there!" said Justin.

"Sometimes it's good to be small," said Mason.

Quotation marks go around words that a character says. Underline the things Mason says in blue. Underline the things Justin says in red.

" "

quotation marks

Mason   Blue

Justin   Red

SKILL Identify who is telling the story

LOOKING FOR A SNACK

A squirrel and a raccoon were sitting on a tree branch. They were hungry.

"Let's find something to eat in the trash can," said Raccoon.

"Ick!" said Squirrel. "I don't want to eat trash. Let's take nuts from the store."

"It's not nice to take things," said Raccoon. Just then, the two saw a girl looking up at them. She put crackers on the ground and backed away. The animals ran down and grabbed the snack. They took it back up to the tree to eat. The girl smiled.

Sometimes parts of a story are filled in by a narrator who isn't one of the characters. In the activity below the narrator is represented by a speech bubble. Show who made each statement by circling the narrator, the raccoon, or the squirrel.

1. It's not nice to take things.

2. The animals ran down and grabbed the snack.

3. Let's take nuts from the store.

4. They were hungry.

SKILL Identify who is telling the story

THE LION AND THE MOUSE

> Draw a line from each statement to the animal or person that those words came from.

Once, a lion trapped a mouse under his paw.

"If you let me go, I will find a way to help you," said the mouse.

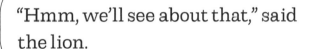

"Hmm, we'll see about that," said the lion.

The lion let the mouse run away. Later, the lion got trapped in a net.

The lion yelled, "Someone, help!"

The mouse came and chewed through all the ropes until the lion could get free.

Narrator

SKILL Identify who is telling the story

CATCHING DINNER

All animals have to find food. Spiders use webs to catch food. First, the spider finds a branch. Then, it spins a sticky thread called silk. It spins many silk threads between the branches. Next, it makes many circles of silk to fill in the web. Last, it waits for a fly to get stuck in the web. Dinnertime!

Mark each sentence below by coloring in the check if it's true, or the X if it's false.

1. Spiders use webs for shelter. ✓ ✗

2. Silk is a sticky thread. ✓ ✗

3. Spiders pull food into their webs. ✓ ✗

4. The first step is for a spider to find a branch. ✓ ✗

SKILL Answer questions about key details

GETTING AROUND IN A CITY

Cities are places where many people live and work close together. There are many ways to get around in a city. Some people walk or ride a bike. People can ride buses or taxis. Some cities have trains above ground for people to ride. Other cities have trains below ground. These are called subways. Some people drive cars to get around the city. It can be hard to find a parking place in a big city!

Underline a detail from the text that supports each statement. Use the colors indicated.

1. Subways are found underground.

2. If you don't have a car, you can still get around in a city.

3. Having a car can be a problem in a city.

4. There are a lot of people in cities.

SKILL Answer questions about key details

PLAYING HOCKEY

Hockey is a sport played on ice. There are two teams with six players each. The game starts when a puck is dropped in the middle of the ice. Both teams use long sticks to hit the puck into their goal. Teams get one point for each goal they make. The team with the most points at the end wins.

Fill in the blanks by writing questions that someone could answer after reading the text. Find someone to read the text and try your questions.

Where _____

_____?

How many _____

_____?

What _____

_____?

SKILL Answer questions about key details

THE AMAZON RAIN FOREST

The Amazon rain forest is hot all year. It gets a lot of rain. Trees, moss, vines, and ferns grow in the Amazon. Many animals live in the Amazon. Some live on the ground. Others live in different levels of the trees. Some are found in water. You can find sloths, alligators, and apes there. The Amazon rain forest is the biggest rain forest in the world. It is an important habitat for many plants and animals.

Complete the crossword below.

1. An Amazon water animal
2. Animals live in different _____ of the trees.
3. It is the _____ rain forest in the world.
4. The temperature in the Amazon

LIVING OR NONLIVING

All things around us are living or nonliving. Living things grow and change. Nonliving things stay the same. All living things use energy. For example, people use food for energy. Some nonliving things use energy. A TV is nonliving and it uses electricity for energy. Other nonliving things don't use energy. A rock doesn't use energy. Living things are made of cells. Nonliving things are not. Can you tell if something is living or nonliving?

This text compares living and nonliving things. Write a fact from the text about living and nonliving things in each of their ovals. Then write a fact from the text about both living and nonliving things where the ovals overlap.

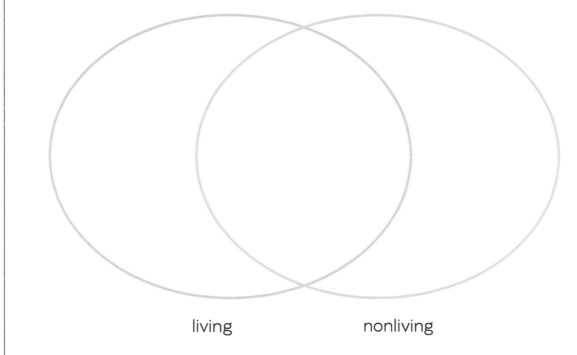

living   nonliving

SKILL Describe the connection between two individuals, events, ideas, or pieces of information

HOW DOES RAIN WORK?

Water is always moving around the earth. Water moves from the earth up to the sky. Water moves up in tiny drops. When these drops get cold, they stick together. This makes a cloud. When a cloud is full of lots of water drops, the drops fall down. When the drops fall down, they help plants grow! Soon the water will move back up to the sky again.

Sometimes one thing makes another thing happen. This is called cause and effect. Draw a line from each cause to its effect.

Cause   **Effect**

SKILL Describe the connection between two individuals, events, ideas, or pieces of information

THE PROBLEM WITH BEARS

Bears live in many national parks where people like to camp and hike. People bring food with them. When bears come looking for the food, they get too close to people. This is dangerous. To keep bears away, park workers put out special trash cans. Bears can't break into these cans. They also have people lock up their food in metal boxes.

This text describes a problem and two ways to solve the problem. Complete the diagram with the problem and the solutions.

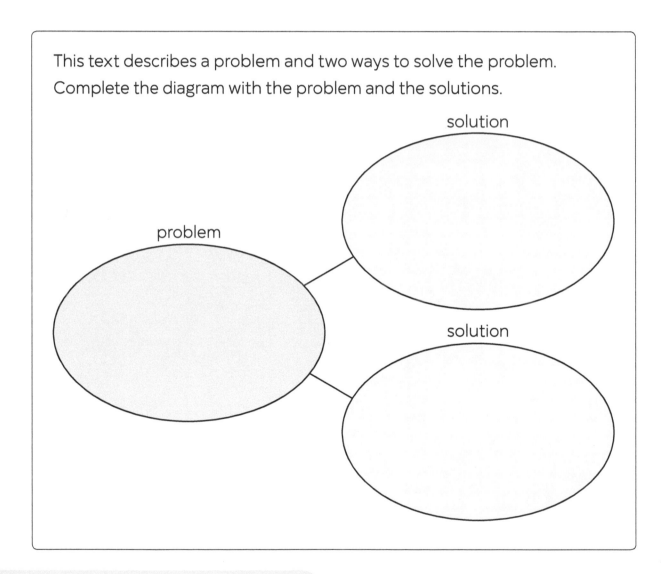

solution

problem

solution

SKILL Describe the connection between two individuals, events, ideas, or pieces of information

HOW TO MAKE PIZZA BAGELS

Ingredients:
bagels
tomato sauce
cheese
pepperoni

1. Preheat the oven to 325 degrees Fahrenheit.

2. Slice the bagels in half and toast them.

3. Put tomato sauce on the bagels.

4. Sprinkle cheese on the bagels.

5. Add pepperoni or any other toppings you like.

6. Put the bagels in the oven for 5 minutes to melt the cheese.

7. Enjoy your pizza bagels!

This recipe shows a sequence of steps. For each pair of steps, circle the one that comes first.

1.

add pepperoni	put tomato sauce on

2.

preheat the oven	sprinkle cheese on

3.

put the bagels in the oven	slice the bagels

4.

toast the bagels	melt the cheese

SKILL Describe the connection between two individuals, events, ideas, or pieces of information

MATCH THE STRUCTURE

Each mini story uses a different structure. Read the text and draw a line to match it with its structure.

Making too much trash is a problem because trash takes up space in landfills. One way to make less trash is to recycle.

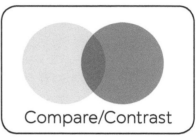

Compare/Contrast

First, put toothpaste on the brush. Then brush it against your teeth. Last, rinse your mouth with water.

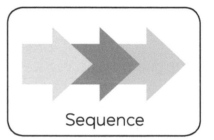

Sequence

Frogs and toads can both live in water or on land. Frogs have smooth skin and toads have bumpy skin.

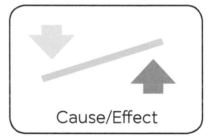

Cause/Effect

When the weather is warm, it causes snow to melt.

Problem/Solution

SKILL Describe the connection between two individuals, events, ideas, or pieces of information

WHAT IS THE TUNDRA?

Read each word below and fill in the stars to show how familiar the word is to you. For words that you are less familiar with, look for clues in the passage about their meaning. If you need more help, ask an adult what they mean.

	NEVER HEARD THIS WORD	HAVE HEARD THIS WORD	KNOW A LITTLE ABOUT IT	CAN EXPLAIN IT TO OTHERS
tundra	☆	☆	☆	☆
permafrost	☆	☆	☆	☆
habitat	☆	☆	☆	☆

There are different **habitats** all over the world. The **tundra** is one kind of **habitat**. It is cold and dry in the **tundra**. If you dig into the ground in the **tundra**, you will find **permafrost**. This is soil that is always frozen. It is hard for plants and animals to live in the **tundra**. Polar bears live in the **tundra** during the summer. The **tundra** is a very harsh **habitat**.

After reading the passage, describe what the tundra is to someone else.

SKILL Ask questions to clarify word and phrase meaning

ELEPHANTS ARE MAMMALS

Elephants are the largest animals that live on land. They are mammals. All mammals are warm-blooded. Warm-blooded animals like elephants make their own body heat by burning food. Mammals have hair. Elephants have only a little bit of hair. Mammals are vertebrates. This means they have a backbone. An elephant's backbone starts at its neck and ends at the tip of its tail. Elephants are very big mammals!

Draw a line to match each word to its meaning. Use clues in the text to help you.

mammal		an animal that makes its own body heat
warm-blooded		an animal with a backbone
vertebrate		an animal that is warm-blooded, has a backbone, and has hair

SKILL Ask questions to clarify word and phrase meaning

PARTS OF A PLANE

Each part of a plane is important. The **fuselage** holds the people or the cargo that the plane is carrying. The **engines** help the plane move fast enough to lift into the air. The **stabilizers** keep the plane from tipping too much. **Ailerons** are the pieces on the tip of each **wing**. They move to help the plane turn. All the parts of a plane work together to take flight!

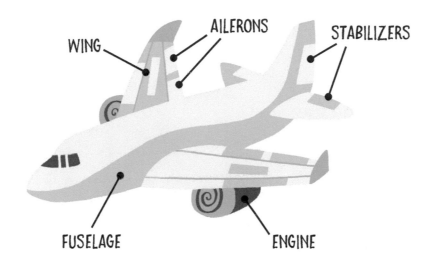

WING   AILERONS   STABILIZERS

FUSELAGE   ENGINE

Use the diagram and clues in the text to figure out the meanings of the bold words. Write them in the blanks where they make sense.

1. The _____ on the wings help turn the plane.

2. The _____ is the main body of the plane.

3. At the back of the plane are the _____ , which help make a smooth ride.

SKILL Ask questions to clarify word and phrase meaning

BEWARE OF BLIZZARDS!

Blizzards are strong snowstorms. They happen when warm, **moist** air meets cold air. For a snowstorm to be a blizzard, it has to also be windy. Wind and snow can cause a **whiteout**. Blizzards can be dangerous because they make it hard to drive. If people go out in a blizzard for too long, they can get **frostbite**. When a blizzard hits, stay inside and stay safe!

Glossary

frostbite: when a body part is damaged from being cold for too long

moist: wet

whiteout: snow falling so heavily that it is hard to see

Use the text and the glossary to decide if each statement below is true or false. If it is true, color the check. If it is false, color the X.

1. Moist air is very dry.

2. Frostbite is caused by polar bears.

3. It is hard to see when there is a whiteout.

4. In this passage, a whiteout is something you use to cover a mistake on paper.

SKILL Ask questions to clarify word and phrase meaning

DOLPHIN CHATTER

Some words have more than one meaning. Good readers think about which meaning makes the most sense with the text. For each bold word below, color the check by the meaning that makes the most sense.

Dolphins make noises to "talk" to other dolphins. They don't say words but they do make **barks** and clicks.	✓ ✓	**bark**: the covering on a tree **bark**: an animal sound
Dolphins can make sounds that rise and **fall**. Each dolphin sounds different.	✓ ✓	**fall**: to go down **fall**: a season
When dolphins make noises, they take **turns**, just like people who are talking.	✓ ✓	**turns**: spinning in circles **turns**: doing the same thing but not at the same time
Dolphins use sounds to tell their **peers** that they are lost, happy, or in danger. These sounds help dolphins work together to survive.	✓ ✓	**peers**: looks at something **peers**: others that are like you

SKILL Ask questions to clarify word and phrase meaning

WHAT'S A CAVITY?

Has a dentist ever told you that you have a cavity? Cavities are small holes in teeth that can get bigger. Cavities start with germs that grow in your mouth. These germs can stick to your teeth. The germs can break your teeth down over time. When you brush your teeth, you get many of the germs off. This is why it is important to brush your teeth twice a day.

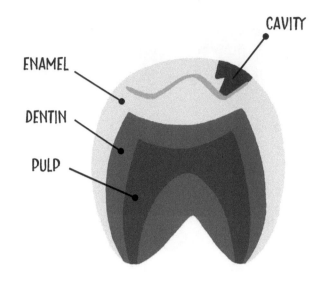

For each fact below, write **T** if the information came from the text. Write **P** if the information came from the picture.

1. Cavities start with germs in your mouth. ____

2. Cavities form in the enamel. ____

3. The inside of a tooth is called pulp. ____

4. Brushing your teeth gets germs off. ____

SKILL Distinguish between information in pictures and information in text

INFORMATION HUNT

TOOL 1

TOOL 3

TOOL 4

Butterflies and Moths

There are a few ways to tell butterflies and moths apart. Butterflies have bright colors and moths have dull colors. The wings of a butterfly fold up high. The wings of a moth fold down over their body. Butterflies usually fly during the day and moths fly at night.

TOOL 2

Time a Monarch Butterfly Spends in Each Life Cycle Phase	
egg	4 days
caterpillar	14 days
chrysalis	10 days
butterfly	28 days

The pictures, table, and text above give different kinds of information about butterflies. Mark the page according to the instructions to show where you would find each piece of information.

1. Write an X next to the tool that shows you what a butterfly looks like.
2. Draw a circle around the tool that shows you where you could go to see butterflies.
3. Draw a line under the tool that tells you how many days a butterfly spends as a chrysalis.
4. Draw an arrow to the tool that helps you tell butterflies and moths apart.

SKILL Distinguish between information in pictures and information in text

KIDS AND PHONES

Kids under ten should not have cell phones. If kids have phones, they will spend too much time on phone games. This means they won't play with friends or be as active. It's dangerous for kids to have cell phones because people they don't know could call them. Parents should wait until kids are older to let them have cell phones.

This text was written to get you to agree with the author's opinion, or point. Underline the first sentence of the reading passage. This is the author's opinion about kids and cell phones. Circle the words below that match how the author would describe phones for kids under ten.

The author would say phones for kids under ten are . . .

dangerous

a bad use of time

helpful

needed

expensive

a bad idea

a good idea

safe

SHOULD BUSES HAVE SEAT BELTS?

Some people think that buses should have seat belts like cars. Seat belts on buses are not a good idea. Buses are made with tall seats to keep kids safe in a crash. Spending extra money on seat belts is not needed. Also, seat belts might be hard for kids to get on and off if they needed to leave the bus quickly. Schools should not spend money on seat belts for buses.

Complete the crossword puzzle.

1. _____ can be hard to take off.
2. Buses have _____ seats.
3. The author thinks seat belts cost too much _____.
4. The author thinks seat belts on buses are a _____ idea.

SKILL Identify the author's point and reasons

DON'T SKIP THIS

If you think skipping breakfast is a good idea, think again. Breakfast is the most important meal because the body has gone a long time without food. It needs food for energy. Eating breakfast helps you think and do your best at school in the morning. Breakfast also helps you stay in a better mood. To have a good morning, take some time to eat breakfast.

Does the author think eating breakfast is important? Talk about it. Circle the pictures that match the reasons the author gives for eating breakfast.

SKILL Identify the author's point and reasons

WHAT GOOD ARE CHORES?

A fact is something that is true and can be proven. An opinion is how someone feels about something. Other people might feel differently. For each statement below, color F if it is a fact or O if it is an opinion.

Examples

Fact: People use water to wash dishes.

Opinion: Washing dishes is too hard for kids.

All kids should have chores.	(F) (O)
Chores are needed to help kids learn things they will need to do as adults.	(F) (O)
Kids can help wash clothes or do yard work.	(F) (O)
Many jobs need to be done each day to keep a family going.	(F) (O)
It's not fair for only the adults in a family to help out.	(F) (O)
Chores are an important part of growing up in a family.	(F) (O)

SKILL Identify the author's point and reasons

Answer Key

Activity 1

1. false, 2. true, 3. true, 4. false

Activity 2

1. Draw an arrow to the pig.
2. Draw a X near the dog.
3. Draw circles around the pig, dog, cat, and hen.
4. Draw a square around the hen.

Activity 3

1. blanket fort, 2. a toy, 3. a boy, 4. imagining

Activity 4

The story is happening at a: *farm*

In the boxes, draw a tractor, a barn, and hay bales. Your answers could vary if you think of other things that you could see at a farm.

Activity 5

1. mirror, 2. dog, 3. one, 4. nice

Activity 6

The three characters are Cam, Jun, and Nan.

Activity 7

Circle the turtle, the snail, the seal, and the crab.

Activity 8

The postcard should include a lake with big rocks and a mountain background.

Activity 9

I wanted to have a *party*. It might get ruined because of the *rain*. I wish the weather was *sunny*.

Activity 10

Draw a line through the following path: star, pine cone, peanut butter, birdseed, string, tree.

Activity 11

E, M, B

Activity 12

Draw these things in order on the path: a park, a bridge, a pond

Activity 13

Color the following path: start, box, scissors, crayon, pillow, finished box

Activity 14

Ben was scared of something *new*. Ben learned that he could be *friends* with a *frog* that was not the *same* as him.

Activity 15

First calendar: Monday— basketball, Tuesday—soccer, Wednesday—jump rope

Second calendar: Monday— soccer, Tuesday—soccer, Wednesday—soccer

Activity 16

Circle the scarf, cheese wedge, mouse, and winter hat

Activity 17

Draw a monster with five eyes, a funny nose, one big foot, funny hair, short arms, three ears, and a skateboard.

Activity 18

Connect the first passage to the picture of the cave, the second passage to the picture of the grocery store, and the third passage to the picture of the rocket and moon

Activity 19

1. Dena, 2. red, 3. dad, 4. five

Activity 20

1. Underline Trey and Bigs in red.
2. Underline "on the couch" in blue.
3. Underline "water" and "food" in green.
4. Underline "wagged his tail" in yellow.

Activity 21

1. false, 2. false, 3. true, 4. true

Activity 22

1. Circle the tree with small apples.
2. Draw an arrow to the tree with big apples.
3. Draw a box around the tree with only branches.
4. Answers will vary.

Activity 23

Draw a pig using the instructions given.

Activity 24

1. ape, 2. bug house, seals, or ape, 3. no, 4. yes

Activity 25

1. Two, 2. chocolate, 3. water, 4. regular milk

Activity 26

Penguins have: feathers, beaks, flippers

Penguins can: eat fish, swim, hatch from eggs

Penguins cannot: fly

Activity 27

Add toes, fingers, and nickels to the web.

Activity 28

adult frog—4, tadpoles—2, eggs—1, tadpoles with legs—3

Activity 29

snowflake—animal tracks; cold temperature—birds flying away; plant with no leaves—animal hibernating

Activity 30

Draw a fireplace, bed, table, door, and windows.

Activity 31

1. snail, 2. six, 3. three, 4. ants

Activity 32

1. Circle the grocery store, the gas station, and the school.
2. Draw a line down the road from the apartments to the school.
3. Draw a box around the park.
4. Draw an arrow to the grocery store and the gas station.

Activity 33

Mark "Weather" in yellow.

Mark "California on a Map" in green.

Mark "California Long Ago" in blue.

Mark "Fun Things to Do" in red.

Activity 34

1. Saturn, 2. rings, 3. moon, 4. sun

Activity 35

1. Circle the eyelashes.
2. Put a check mark by the pupil and iris.
3. Put an X by the eyelid.
4. Draw a box around the iris.

Activity 36

Answers will vary.

Activity 37

After reading:

Ladybugs have: wings, six legs, mouths, shells, spots

Ladybugs can: crawl, fly

Ladybugs eat: other insects, plants

Activity 38

After reading:

1. true, 2. false, 3. false, 4. true

Activity 39

Answers will vary.

Activity 40

Answers will vary.

Activity 41

Answers will vary.

Activity 42

1. smiled, 2. Wes, 3. mom, 4. bowl

Activity 43

Fill in the smiley faces by:

The rabbit is Trina's favorite toy.

The rabbit is getting dirty.

Grandma washed the rabbit while Trina was asleep.

Activity 44

1. ant, 2. ant, 3. snail, 4. snail

Activity 45

1. Circle the mask.
2. Draw a box around the boots and shirt.
3. Draw an arrow to the hat and wings.
4. Answers will vary.

Activity 46

Draw a girl up in a tree pushing the branch down.

Activity 47

Write something like "play with others" or "get ideas from other people" in the blank.

Activity 48

girl looking nervous—2, girl dancing—4, stage—1, girl taking a breath—3

Activity 49

1. boy with a bowl, 2. girl with a pan, 3. boy with spoons, 4. dad

Activity 50

1. true, 2. true, 3. false, 4. false

Activity 51

Draw a table, a rug, and a fireplace.

Activity 52

1. Underline "Manny helps his team" or "Manny says, 'Good game!'" in red.
2. Underline "Manny plays football with his team every Saturday" or "Manny runs as fast as he can" in green.
3. Underline "Manny says, 'Good game!'" in yellow.
4. Underline "Manny runs as fast as he can" or "Manny helps his team" in blue.

Activity 53

The problem is that Allie *doesn't like waiting*.

To help make the waiting easier, Allie's mom *plays a game with her*.

Activity 54

The character who runs into a problem in the story: Kevin

The character whose feelings we know the most about: Kevin

The character whose feelings change: Kevin

Activity 55

Beginning: circle sad and unimportant

End: circle helpful, important, and needed

Activity 56

Underline "Pop! Pop! Pop!" "Click!" "Tap, tap, tap" and "Shhhh!" in red.

Underline "Squish!" and "fuzzy blanket" in blue.

Underline "The room is dark" and "The movie turns on" in green.

Activity 57

Answers will vary.

Activity 58

Color the smiley faces for: scared, bored, and excited.

Activity 59

"I am soft . . ."—pillow

"I am sweet . . ."—cake

"I am round . . ."—soccer ball

"I am cold . . ."—icicles

"I am small . . ."—bird

Activity 60

Things you can imagine seeing: street, kids, yellow lights, bus

Things you can imagine hearing: birds, the bus stopping, the doors opening, feet stomping

Things you can imagine feeling: cool air, stomping up stairs

Activity 61

1. boys, 2. painting, 3. animals, 4. green

Activity 62

On Keesha's pizza, draw sauce, cheese, pepperoni, and mushrooms.

On Rita's pizza, draw sauce, cheese, sausage, and peppers.

Activity 63

Omar says something like, "I felt excited because I got a prize."

Shelby says something like, "I felt sad because I didn't get a prize."

Activity 64

Faith: younger, shares about school, pulls weeds

Mrs. Conway: older, shares about grandkids, waters plants

Both: live on the same street, work in the garden, like sharing stories

Activity 65

Color the following path: start, knife, spoon, marker, knife, candle, jack-o'-lantern

Activity 66

1. Circle the mouse, squirrel, raccoon, and dog.
2. Circle the dog.
3. Circle the squirrel and raccoon.
4. Circle the mouse and raccoon.

Activity 67

Needs: food, clothes, shelter

Wants: games, candy, toys

Activity 68

1. false, 2. true, 3. true, 4. false

Activity 69

1. covered, 2. stone, 3. long, 4. bones

Activity 70

Dirt bikes is underlined the most times.

Activity 71

Main topic: *baseball*

Nine players from one team play in the field.

The field is *diamond*-shaped.

One team tries to hit the ball. The other team tries to *catch* the ball.

Activity 72

false, true, true, false, true, false, true

Activity 73

1. minus, 2. star, 3. star, 4. minus

Activity 74

Weather, Wildlife, Plants

Activity 75

1. pages 7 and 29
2. page 31
3. page 4
4. page 19

Activity 76

crust: the top layer of rock

landslide: the rocks and dirt coming down the side of the volcano

eruption: the ash and magma shooting from the top of the volcano

magma: the lava underground

Activity 77

Circle "Hours" in yellow.

Circle "Locations" in blue.

Circle "Homework Help" in red.

Circle "Contact Us" in green.

Activity 78

Butterflies and Their Food: check butterflies, how butterflies eat, shows one thing a butterfly does

Butterfly Life Cycle: check butterflies, how butterflies change, shows how a butterfly changes

Activity 79

Things to Do in Colorado

Circle "Colorado" in red.

Underline Rocky Mountains in green.

Underline any other fact unique to the passage in blue.

Colorado's Mountains

Circle "Colorado" in red.

Underline Rocky Mountains in green.

Underline any other fact unique to the passage in blue.

Activity 80

Left side: "Skulls protect brains."

Center: "Topic: bones"

Right side: "Bones give us shape."

Activity 81

Answers will vary.

Activity 82

1. money, 2. driveway, 3. lines, 4. chalk

Activity 83

1. false, 2. true, 3. false, 4. true

Activity 84

1—Rosy the parrot, 2—a cookie, 3—the cage, 4—a wooden bar

Activity 85

Beginning: The emperor gives each child a seed to grow.

Middle: Chen tries to grow the seed but it won't grow.

End: Chen becomes the emperor because he is honest.

Characters: The emperor, Chen, other children

Setting: Long ago in China

Lesson: It is best to be honest.

Activity 86

Somebody: Dante

Wanted: to give his mom a gift.

But: he didn't have money.

So: he learned to make paper cranes and gave those to his mom.

Activity 87

At first, I was sad because *my poster wasn't perfect.*

Later, I realized that *people would still like it anyway.*

Activity 88

Color the following path: Penny, missing tooth, scared girl, tooth in apple

Activity 89

I wanted to go to the party and the *game*.

It was *hard* to make the choice.

I picked the *party* because it was important to *be with Mario.*

Activity 90

Characters: the narrator (a kid), dad

Setting: in an apartment

Problem: The kid can't find something purple.

Solution: The kid uses the purple nail polish on their hands.

Activity 91

Fairy says, "Magic pot, grow me a rose."—*a rose grows.*

Fairy claps twice—rose stops growing.

Lily says, "Magic pot, grow me a grapevine."—*a grapevine grows.*

Activity 92

The postcard should show a red rock, two craters, a red sandpit, and a school.

Activity 93

Check off: characters, a setting, a problem and solution, and something make believe

Activity 94

Check off: about real things, facts, explains something, text features

Activity 95

"The dragon said . . ."—story

"Bananas . . ."—informational

"Fish and frogs . . ."—informational

"Once there was a girl . . ."—story

"Someone broke . . ."—story

"Bears can eat . . ."—informational

"Hockey . . ."—informational

"Hazel's team . . ."—story

Activity 96

How to Paint a Room: Teaches Something, True Information

The Paint Monster: Silliest, Tells a Story

Activity 97

Draw a person for the first story and a worm for the second story.

Activity 98

Underline in blue:
"Sure!" "I'm right here!"
"Sometimes it's good to be small."

Underline in red:
"Come play hide-and-seek with me" "One, two, three . . ."
"I give up! Where are you?"
"I didn't think anyone could fit back there!"

Activity 99

1. Raccoon, 2. narrator, 3. Squirrel, 4. narrator

Activity 100

narrator, mouse, lion, narrator, lion, narrator

Activity 101

1. false, 2. true, 3. false, 4. true

Activity 102

1. Underline "Other cities have trains below ground. These are called subways" in yellow.
2. Underline "bike," "buses or taxis," and "trains" in blue.
3. Underline "It can be hard to find a parking place" in red.
4. Underline "Cities are places where many people live" in green.

Activity 103

Answers will vary.

Activity 104

1. alligator, 2. levels, 3. biggest, 4. hot

Activity 105

living: grow and change, made of cells

both: use energy

nonliving: stay the same, not made of cells

Activity 106

rain—flower

evaporation—cloud

condensation—rain

Activity 107

problem: bears get too close to people in national parks

solution: special trash cans

solution: special boxes for food

Activity 108

1. put tomato sauce on
2. preheat the oven
3. slice the bagels
4. toast the bagels

Activity 109

"Making too much trash ..."—
problem/solution

"First, put toothpaste ..."—
sequence

"Frogs and toads ..."—
compare/contrast

"When the weather ..."—
cause/effect

Activity 110

Answers will vary.

Activity 111

mammal—an animal that is
warm-blooded, has a backbone,
and has hair

warm-blooded—an animal that
makes its own body heat

vertebrate—an animal with a
backbone

Activity 112

1. ailerons
2. fuselage
3. stabilizers

Activity 113

1. false, 2. false, 3. true, 4. false

Activity 114

bark: an animal sound

fall: to go down

turns: doing the same thing but
not at the same time

peers: others that are like you

Activity 115

1. T, 2. P, 3. P, 4. T

Activity 116

1. Draw an X next to the
   butterfly picture.
2. Draw a circle around the map.
3. Draw a line under the table.
4. Draw an arrow to the text.

Activity 117

Circle: dangerous, a bad use of
time, a bad idea

Activity 118

1. seat belts, 2. tall,
3. money, 4. bad

Activity 119

Circle the brain, the happy face,
and the person running.

Activity 120

opinion, opinion, fact,
fact, opinion, opinion

Skills Index and Common Core Correlations

RL.1.3: Describe characters, settings, and major events in a story, using key details.

RL.1.4: Identify words and phrases in stories or poems that suggest feelings or appeal to the senses.

RL.1.5: Explain major differences between books that tell stories and books that give information, drawing on a wide reading of a range of text types.

RL.1.6: Identify who is telling the story at various points in a text.

RL.1.7: Use illustrations and details in a story to describe its characters, setting, or events.

RL.1.9: Compare and contrast the adventures and experiences of characters in stories.

Activate prior knowledge

Make connections to self and the world

RI.1.1: Ask and answer questions about key details in a text.

Activity 26: All About Penguins

Activity 27: Counting by Fives

Activity 28: Frogs Grow Up

Activity 29: Animals in the Winter

Activity 30: Life in a Log Cabin

Activity 65: How to Carve a Pumpkin

Activity 66: City Animals

Activity 67: Needs and Wants

Activity 68: Taking Care of a Cactus

Activity 69: All about Fossils

Activity 101: Catching Dinner

Activity 102: Getting Around in a City

Activity 103: Playing Hockey

Activity 104: The Amazon Rain Forest

RI.1.2: Identify the main topic and retell key details of a text.

Activity 70: Fun in the Dirt

Activity 71: America's Pastime

Activity 72: Firefighters Working

Activity 73: Ants All Around

RI.1.3 Describe the connection between two individuals, events, ideas, or pieces of information in a text.

Activity 105: Living or Nonliving

Activity 106: How Does Rain Work?

Activity 107: The Problem with Bears

Activity 108: How to Make Pizza Bagels

Activity 109: Match the Structure

RI.1.4: Ask and answer questions to help determine or clarify the meaning of words and phrases in a text.

Activity 110: What Is the Tundra?

Activity 111: Elephants Are Mammals

Activity 112: Parts of a Plane

Activity 113: Beware of Blizzards!

Activity 114: Dolphin Chatter

RI.1.5: Know and use various text features (e.g., headings, tables of contents, glossaries, electronic menus, icons) to locate key facts or information in a text.

Activity 31: Alive in the Yard

Activity 32: The Green Hill Neighborhood

Activity 33: Where Would You Look?

Activity 34: Outer Space

Activity 35: All About Eyes

Activity 74: The Desert

Activity 75: Ocean Index

Activity 76: Volcanoes

Activity 77: The Westwood Libraries Website

RI.1.6 Distinguish between information provided by pictures or other illustrations and information provided by the words in a text.

Activity 115: What's a Cavity?

Activity 116: Information Hunt

RI.1.7: Use the illustrations and details in a text to describe its key ideas.

Activity 21: All About Grasshoppers

Activity 22: Apple Tree All Year

Activity 23: Draw Along

Activity 24: Zoo Trip

Activity 25: What's in Your Cup?

RI.1.8 Identify the reasons an author gives to support points in a text.

Activity 117: Kids and Phones

Activity 118: Should Buses Have Seat Belts?

Activity 119: Don't Skip This

Activity 120: What Good Are Chores?

RI.1.9: Identify basic similarities in and differences between two texts on the same topic (e.g., in illustrations, descriptions, or procedures).

Activity 78: Butterfly Basics

Activity 79: Colorful Colorado

Activity 80: A Look at Bones

About the Author

 **Hannah Braun** writes curriculum for teachers and parents of elementary-aged children. She spent eight years as a classroom teacher and has two children of her own. Hannah loves to bring about "A-ha!" moments for kids by breaking down tricky concepts into digestible parts. She holds a bachelor's degree in elementary education and a master's degree in early childhood education. Hannah is the author of the blog *The Classroom Key* (TheClassroomKey.com), where she shares ideas and information about best practices in teaching. In her free time, Hannah enjoys painting, fitness classes, and playing the French horn in community bands. Follow her on Facebook and Instagram, both @TheClassroomKey.